CODE
RED

A GIFT FROM BEYOND

Marjorie Widmer

Editor: Karen Rowe, www.karenrowe.com

Cover Design: Shake Creative, ShakeTampa.com

Inside Layout: Ljiljana Pavkov

Printed in Canada

ISBN: 978-1-9995689-1-7 (paperback)

ISBN: 978-1-9995689-0-0 (ebook)

This book is dedicated to our beloved son, Cody. Had it not been for that fateful day that we lost him, this book would not have come into being. We were truly blessed to have had such a loving son. Our time together was much too short but, oh, so special. I know we will be together again one day and finally, I will get another Cody hug.

Love You

Mama Bear

Acknowledgements

I would like to acknowledge the enormous help given to me in creating this book. I wish to thank Shelley Shahanaghi. Without her help, this book would never have been written. For their encouragement and guidance I wish to thank Louise, Milada, Johanne, Linda, Stacy, and Cindy.

Also special thanks to my editors, Karen Rowe and Liberty Forrest for handling this project with just the right touch.

Mostly I wish to thank my husband, Kerry and my daughter Kalie who often believed in me more than I did myself. Love you both so much.

Table of Contents

CODE
RED

Introduction

My son, Cody James Arthur, or as most of us called him, "Code," insisted that I had a purpose, and that I was to write this book. His request came after his passing and through Shelley, a life coach who is able to communicate with spirits, and who has helped him to communicate with me. He said that he has meaningful and inspiring information to share with others through me.

My pain of losing Code had been holding me back from receiving his messages. He stated that if I could release the pain, he would be able to talk to me more easily.

Because of Code's messages, now I know that when we die, our spirits are still very much alive. Only our bodies pass away. He has also explained that some souls are more elevated than others. I know some people believe that when you die, your soul goes to heaven and that is it. But since losing Code and hearing what he has shared through Shelley, it has made me question this.

Shelley said he is doing really well and reminds her of a puppy that just got a new home. Through her, Code said to me, "Don't be sad, Mom. I'm in such a good place. It's like the best video game ever. I'm having a blast. I'm happy. There is no pain, no sadness; it is only good here. And there is a bigger message."

One of the most important messages he wanted me to pass along to everyone is to believe in life after death. Cody explained that in heaven there is different light. He emphasized that you do not want to go into the blackness. Grey was for those who want to believe but are not sure, and light was for people who believe in life after death.

He wanted to get the message out to everyone that this life is nothing compared to what is to come. Heaven is real and offers the best of everything. Given the chance, our loved ones in spirit would not want to come back to this life.

First, I must make it clear that I'm not forcing my beliefs onto anyone. What you believe is your business. I'm just sharing what I have found to be true for me, not just because of my own beliefs but because of the messages I have received from Code.

Before he passed, I didn't realize that the spirits of our loved ones had the ability to come and comfort us or that they are with us. But because of my family's experiences since we lost Code, I know I must pass along my daugher, Kalie, my husband Kerry and I have learned.

Everything happens for a reason. There are no coincidences, and we may not know why something happens the way it does but it was meant to be. One day, we will know the reason. If not in this life, we will know when we get to heaven.

Code said that we should celebrate when a loved one dies because that person is born into heaven. It's like another birthday and for this we should celebrate their lives instead of mourning for them, as they are going to a better place. But they do understand our sadness and their spirits are with us to comfort us.

It's hard to say good-bye to the people we love, whether it's a child or a loving spouse of many years. Although we miss them, we should be grateful for the time we have had with them. I know it never seems enough. I've had to remind myself of this, too. We always want more time with them. We aren't ready to have them leave us, and especially as parents we always think we will go before our children; at least, we hope for this. Sadly, as we all know, this is not always the case.

But now, since losing Cody it has been such a comfort to know that we will see our son again. He has told us that death is not the end but the beginning. Not everyone believes and therefore, so many people are hurting over losing loved ones. It is sad to think so many people are heartbroken. If only they realized that their loved ones are still with them, it would be so comforting. All we have to do is look and be open to receiving the signs that they are giving us and we will know they're still nearby.

I know for myself, I don't think I would be where I am today had it not been for Shelley. She made me aware that Cody is not gone; he is still here in spirit. I just had to realize that I was not imagining things and that he was, indeed, trying to bring me comfort.

My family and I have so much for which to be thankful. *I'm so glad, Lord, that you have my son. Thank you for almost twenty-two wonderful years with him. Give me wisdom to pass onto others.*

The Worst News of My Life

❧❦❧

Cody was our son. He passed away suddenly on June 14, 2015. It was undoubtedly the worst day of my life.

We were having supper at my sister Shirley's house, along with four of my five brothers and their families when we saw the police car coming up the driveway. I don't know why I went to answer the door along with my brother-in-law, Stan, but I just felt as though it had to do with me.

The police officer asked if he could talk to me privately. He, Stan and I went over to our house, which was across the driveway. Once inside, the police officer said to me, "I have some bad news to give you. Your son, Cody, was found unresponsive this morning."

I looked at him, confused. "I don't know what you mean," I said, puzzled.

He replied, "Your son passed away this morning."

I went into shock. "No, this can't be! Cody always phones me on Sunday nights. I'm expecting a call from him now. *Please, Lord!*" I begged. *"Don't take my son from me!"*

My husband, Kerry, came into the house at that time and asked what was going on. I cried, "We've lost Code!"

In those first moments, everything was a blur. The next thing I knew, my best friend, Louise, was running in the house and grabbing me. "What's going on?" she asked, obviously concerned.

I just hugged her and cried. "We've lost Code!" Apparently, Kerry had called her and without offering an explanation, he had simply said, "We need you now."

With Louise's help, we got some details from the police officer and were able to make some calls. We called Kerry's brother, Randy, and his wife, Rosina, who asked us to come over to their house in Okotoks, AB.

Kerry and I hopped into the car and off to Okotoks we went. I will never forget our drive through the National Park. We were both crying and so upset. As we were driving, it was cloudy and the sky was grey. All of a sudden, a ray of sunshine streamed into our car, yet nowhere else was there any sun.

I remember saying to Kerry, "Code is letting us know he is in heaven."

A sense of peace came over us. It was like something we had never experienced before.

Throughout the drive, my husband and I continued talking about Code. Kerry asked a certain question regarding Code that had to do with a private conversation between my son and me. I had to be careful how to answer so as not to break Code's confidence. But as soon as Kerry asked the question, my cell phone went *Ping!*

We were in the National Park and there is no cell service, nothing that would make the cell phone go off. I looked at my phone and I knew without a doubt that the "ping" had been from Code. I could just feel him. That was the first of many signs from him.

After arriving at Randy and Rosina's house, our first thought was Kalie, Code's best friend and sister, who was hiking up in Kananaskis, Alberta. She and Code had always had a special bond. She had a nickname for him, "Seige," and he would not let anyone else call him that. It was something special between the two of them. Once, I made the mistake of using it and he said, "No one, but *no one*, calls me this but Kalie!"

The next day was going to be the second worst day of my life, as we had to share this terrible news with her. I wanted to make sure we were the ones who told her what had happened to her brother. We didn't want her to hear it from social media. As she was up in the mountains, I knew her cell phone would not work but as soon as she got down from the mountain and turned on her phone, the news would be all over it.

We had a sleepless night. Kerry and I watched the sun come up, dreading the day ahead, knowing we had to give Kalie the tragic news of her brother's death.

Friends of ours had got in touch with Parks Canada to let them know there had been a family emergency. We asked them if they could tell us where Kalie had parked her car, and to keep an eye on her to get down from the mountain safely but not to tell her anything.

I am so grateful for that day. We walked and waited for Kalie to come, which took a few hours. This gave us time to come to terms with the news as much as was possible. The best way I can describe it was a feeling of peace.

While we were waiting there for Kalie, I wrote Code's eulogy. The words and all I wanted to say came easily to me. I think Code was helping me.

Eventually, we saw Kalie and her partner, Greig, from across the lake and making their way down. When Kalie saw us, she could tell I was upset. She thought it was that her Granny, my mom, had passed. I shook my head and from the look on my face, she just knew. She screamed, "No!"

That is one of the hardest things I have ever had to do. How do you comfort your daughter who has lost her brother and best friend?

On recalling these worst days of my life, my mind drifts to one of the best. It was the day I gave birth to Code, although he made a rather dramatic entrance. The umbilical cord was wrapped around his neck and he was stuck in the birth canal. The doctor shouted at me, "Get him out now!" She used the forceps to pull him out. He stopped breathing twice and we thought for sure we had lost him. Finally, and with great relief we heard him cry.

Code was born with double scoliosis, a curvature of the spine. In his case, his spine was in the shape of an "S". No one knows what causes scoliosis, but I have always wondered if in Code's case, it had been the result of the doctor pulling on him so hard during his birth.

Code's scoliosis didn't appear until he was about thirteen years old. He had come home from a basketball trip complaining of a sore back and asked me to give him a back rub. I took one look at his back and told him that we needed to see a chiropractor, as I thought that his back was out. The chiropractor examined him and explained that we needed to see a doctor, which we did.

The doctor then sent us to the Children's Hospital to see a specialist for back problems. The specialist explained to Code that he would always have scoliosis but as long as he took care of himself, didn't gain a lot of weight, and kept a tight core, he wouldn't need surgery. So Code took care to follow the doctor's orders and worked out regularly to stay in shape.

Because of his back problems, he was in constant pain but he never complained. He had always been a hard worker and that was what got him through it.

None of us knew it but as the scoliosis worsened, Code's spine was damaging his heart. Ultimately, it became enlarged, which led to us losing him. On learning the cause of his death, we were all in shock.

At the time of his death, Code was living in Sylvan Lake, working in the oil field as a pipefitter. We had always had to encourage Code to go to high school. For him, the only reason he went was to be with his friends, but school was not his thing. All of that changed once he found what he liked to do, which was welding and pipefitting. Adding to his joy, he loved working with all the guys at NTL and Cords and the feeling was mutual.

His cousin, Ryan, was like a big brother to our son and had got Code into this line of work. He told us that when it came to the work, there was nothing that Code wasn't able to do. Apparently, he was just a natural. As of this writing, Ryan still hasn't been able to find any-one who comes close to doing the job as well as Code had done it.

Code was so excited to have gotten an apprenticeship. I had called him the Friday night before he passed away and said, "You did it, Code! You've been accepted to trade school! We are so proud of you!"

He replied, "Mom, can you believe it? I'm actually excited to go to school!"

Those words had been music to my ears.

The day after we gave Kalie the awful news of his pass-ing, she, Kerry, and I went up to Sylvan Lake to meet with the RMCP. The police officer that met us was one of the ones who had attended to Code when he passed. He told us, "I've got to let you know that your son looked so peaceful. He was lying on the couch the same way I do. He had one arm above his head and there was nothing that would suggest anything was wrong.

"I had the pleasure of meeting your son last winter. It was a snowy morning, February 14th, and Code had put his truck in the ditch. He was in the process of digging himself out."

The policeman told us that they had ended up sitting on Code's tailgate and having a great talk about life.

"Your son was a stand-up young man. I'm so sorry for your loss," he offered sincerely.

The police had taken a box from Code's apartment. In it were knives, axes and swords. Code had a thing for these treasures, especially knives. That was the best gift you could give him.

"Wow!" the police officer exclaimed. "He sure has some unusual collections!"

After we met with the police, we went over to Code's apartment. When we pulled up, we knew right away which apartment was his. On his balcony was the gravity chair we had just given him for an early birthday present. Next to the chair was an MGD beer, his favourite.

Kalie and I went into his apartment and straight to his bedroom closet. We started grabbing his shirts and his housecoat. We closed our eyes, remembering Code and burying our noses in his clothing, wanting to smell him. It is amazing how scents bring back memories, and Code had always smelled so good.

Kalie wanted his housecoat. She cried, saying that when she had it on it was like getting a Cody hug. I got his famous "Wilmer Tux," his favourite green plaid jacket. We chose the clothes we thought would make him look good for his service, knowing he would want that.

The next day we had to go to the funeral home to make the arrangements. This was so hard to do. We were still in shock and not ready to think about our loss but we had to deal with it.

The funeral home put us in a room, explaining that they were getting Code prepared for us. Kalie asked if she could go last and wanted to go in by herself. Into the viewing room Kerry and I went. At the far end, I could see Code lying in the coffin. This memory still brings tears to my eyes. I started crying and touched his face. I rubbed his cheek and whiskers. To my amazement, I saw a tear in Code's eye. I knew he was also crying to see his Dad and me so broken. I will always remember that tear and how special it was.

A Life Well-Lived

When we got home from the funeral home, I got a phone call from Code's special friend, Naomerzz, asking if a few of his friends could come up to see us. I cried, "We would love for you to come!" What a wonderful surprise when into the house came about twenty of Code's good friends carrying flowers and food. All of us sat out on the deck telling stories of good times with Code. Sometimes we cried and at other times we were laughing. This was so special to us.

Code's friends were also good at helping us get things ready for his service. I think they needed to keep busy, too. Kerry had no problem finding jobs for them to do. We were grateful for their help, but even more so for their presence, a beautiful reminder of our beloved son's precious life.

It seems like only yesterday that Code graduated. The grad class had a bush party up above the town of Wilmer, like they do every year. Code had given me a phone call the next morning, asking if he and some of his friends could come for breakfast. I replied, "No problem, come on down."

A few minutes later, I received another phone call asking how many friends he was allowed to bring. I laughed, "Code, bring whoever wants to come!"

It's a good thing that I always have lots of food on hand. We ended up needing to feed about twenty hungry teenagers on the spur of the moment.

Kerry got into the swing of things. He got the BBQ going and the music cranked up. I remember Kalie telling me later that Code had said he was so proud to call us his Mom and Dad. He loved that we had no problem welcoming a large group of his friends into our home and feeding them at a moment's notice.

I remember my friend, Louise, telling me that only God's chosen ones die on Sundays. Both of us had lost our fathers on Sundays and I lost my son on a Sunday, too. I have so many questions for the good Lord, like "Why my son?" I'm sure that this is the first of many questions parents would have for the Lord. "Why did you choose my child?"

Code had always said we had the perfect family. Sure, we had our ups and downs but we had so much love. I always said to the kids that we were rich in love if not in money. We had some amazing holidays together, and the kids were always willing to try different things, like snorkelling, scuba diving and cliff-jumping. Neither one of them had any fear and if one did something, the other would follow, or they would go hand-in-hand.

One of the greatest treasures I have is a video of Kalie and Code holding hands and jumping off the cliff at Twin

Lake. It is priceless as Kalie accidently kicks Code "where it counts" and he hollers. But apart from that moment in the video, they are having fun and smiling, and that always makes me smile, too.

Code had worked at Napa Auto Parts for four years. He absolutely loved that job. He took such pleasure when the men would come into the store and visit. They always treated him like one of them.

Code had always wanted a truck and he saved his money till he was able to pay cash for one of his own. And what a truck it was, his beloved "Code Red." It was a big red Dodge 4X4. I have never seen anyone as proud as Code was when he got that truck. He had the biggest smile on his face when he showed it to his Dad and me. I will also never forget my first ride in it. The music was cranked up and he wanted to impress me, which he did.

We went through the town of Wilmer and up to Munn Lake, with both of us laughing. I told him that it was the greatest truck ever.

That truck saw many happy times. There was nothing our son loved more than driving his friends around in Code Red. He would get a phone call at 3 a.m. from one friend or another who needed a ride home and off he would go. I don't think he ever turned down a friend.

It was our son's beloved Code Red and not a hearse that took him for his last ride. We thought that this would be exactly the way he would want to leave us. One of his best friends drove and Kalie rode shotgun.

I got up early the morning after we got back from picking up Code's truck and bringing it back home from Sylvan Lake. I looked out the kitchen window to see it, knowing that I would never again see his smiling face while he drove it, which was just about more than I could bear.

Just then, Kerry walked into the kitchen, first seeing me and then seeing the truck. We hugged each other and sobbed. Prior to losing our son, seeing the truck outside our home had always brought us comfort knowing Code was safe with us. To think he was never coming home again was heartbreaking.

Later, I told my sister, Shirley, about our bittersweet moment with the truck that morning. She said that at that very moment, she had looked outside. Appearing over the hayfields right where we were looking at Code's truck was the most beautiful rainbow, and with colours she had never seen before. I know this was Code trying to bring comfort to his Dad and me. He wanted to let us know that he was in heaven. He wanted us to be happy for him and not to be sad.

In those earliest days and many others that followed, I didn't think I would survive the loss; the pain was unbearable. I didn't want to live without Code. Then I remembered that there were other people who still needed me. My first thought was my daughter, Kalie, and how much she was going to need Kerry and me. I could never leave her. That just wouldn't have been fair to her.

I think she has suffered more than anyone. I have Kerry but it had always been "Kalie and Code," the two of them a team, and now Kalie is on her own. This is the only time I have regretted not having more children. It would have been so much easier for Kalie if she'd had a brother or sister, if she could have talked to another sibling. It was up to Kerry and me as her parents to help her through the grieving process in any way we could. I'm also very grateful for her partner, Greig, who has been so supportive.

I ran into the lady who had bought our house in Windermere where we used to live. That home held some very special memories as we lived there for most of the kids' lives. She told me that Kalie had paid her a visit. She explained that she had looked out her front window one day and had seen a parked car with a very upset young woman inside. When she went out to see what was going on, Kalie told her that we used to live there. She started to cry, saying she had just lost her brother.

The woman let Kalie go into the bedroom where I had marked on the wall in the closet how much both Kalie and Code had grown. Then they found the place in the concrete where both our children had left their handprints. Kalie got to walk through the house recalling many memories of happier days. The lady told me that she could feel the love Kalie had for her brother.

At Code's service, there were about three hundred people. At the end of the service, we were getting Code Red ready when Kerry came to me and said, "Marj, there is someone I'd like you to meet."

I looked at the young man with him and I responded, "Sorry, but I can't place you."

He replied that he was Code's boss from Cords in Blackfalds, Alberta. "I just had to come and tell you what a great son you had," he said. "Code was such a hard worker and a friend to all. He always talked about three things: his family, the farm and his mountains." This made me so proud of Code.

Learning to Cope

During preparations for the service and making all the arrangements as well as handling Code's affairs, we had been on autopilot. Grateful that we had been kept so busy, we hadn't had much time to think about our loss. It had given our brains and hearts a break because it had all been too much to take in.

I found myself dealing with the grief of losing Code by pretending that he was still at work and that everything was normal. I couldn't bear the thought of him being gone. I remember telling this to my brother-in-law, Stan, who lives next door to us. He told me he was doing the same thing because Code had been like a son to him.

Little by little, I let reality in, but when it got too painful I would try to block out the truth. I would walk into Code's bedroom and look at his belongings including all of his Fox caps that he was so proud of and that he loved. I kept saying to myself, "This can't be happening. I'm going to wake up and Code is still going to be with

us. I'm going to get a phone call and hear, 'Hey, Mom!'"
How I had always loved hearing that…

I remember thinking, 'Now he's everywhere but
nowhere.'

I took six weeks off from work when we lost Code.
Kalie and I spent a lot of time together talking. We went
camping for a week, played cards and took lots of walks.
I would read books and try to get into the stories, anything to take my mind off my loss. Several people gave
me books on how to deal with grief and I found most
of them were very depressing. The books were telling
me that I should feel this way or that way, which wasn't
helpful. I think everyone has to find his or her own way
of dealing with grief. There is no "right way."

In time, I found that when I exercised, I would feel
better. And I discovered that if I spent too much time
inside the house, I would go crazy. I took lots of walks
and got fresh air.

I must say, there was one book about signs from your
loved ones that made me feel better. Prior to that, there
had been times I wondered if Code was trying to let me
know that he was with me, but I thought I was imagining
things. This was before I met Shelley and she validated
that the signs I thought I had been receiving were truly
from Code.

I always had trouble at night and would cry, but sometimes I could feel a weight at the end of my bed. It was
as though someone was sitting down and then I would
feel my spirits being lifted. I knew without a doubt that
it was Code coming for a visit and trying to comfort me.

I kept myself as busy as possible by going back to work and diving into my life again. I tried to work myself to exhaustion so that when I went to bed, I could sleep. But I always seemed to wake up at 3 a.m. At times, I would get up and walk around. I didn't know why, or what I was looking for at the time. Then I would get a sign from Code that made me feel better and I could go back to bed. Shelley suggested that I had probably been looking for that sign without being consciously aware of it. Having her tell me this was very healing.

Not long after Code passed, a friend came to visit me. She had lost her son a number of years earlier. She asked me to call her any time if I wanted to talk or to have coffee. She had said, "For a while you'll be busy but it will hit you and if you need to talk to someone who has dealt with a loss like this, call."

She had also explained, "You will run into different people, the ones who want to talk and feel comfortable around you, and the others who will turn from you. I would be walking down the street and people would cross in front of me so they wouldn't have to face me."

It had felt so good talking to someone who had gone through a loss like this; no one could truly understand exactly what I was going through except another mother who had lost a child. I was also glad to be prepared for how some people might react to me.

And then it started happening, just as she had predicted. I remember going to a farmer's market to get some veggies and I saw a friend I had known for years. In the past, we would always joke and talk but that time he ignored me and turned away. Some people turned around, as if not knowing what to say. Still others, including people I didn't know well at all, came right up to me and asked if they could give me a hug. I would be at work and sometimes people wouldn't say anything at all but would just come up and squeeze my hand to let me know they cared.

In general, the valley where we live has been really supportive of us since we lost Code. Having lived here all of my life, I know a lot of people in the area and most knew Code or had heard of him.

Soon I was discovering other parents who had lost children. I was surprised at how many there were. I found comfort in talking with them, I suppose at least in part because of the knowledge that if they had survived their loss, I would find a way, too.

I started making notes about my conversations with them and about how each person had dealt with the loss. From those discussions, it seemed that grieving parents' biggest fear was that their children would be forgotten. Some people think it might be better for the parents to stop talking about their children and get on with their lives but that is exactly what they *don't* want to do.

When our loved ones die, we want to keep our memories of them alive by having conversations about them. They are still parts of our lives. They're what make us who we are as people. One friend came up to me to say how sorry he was about the news of Code. I started to cry and he apologized for mentioning it. I replied, "I may cry when you talk about him but I would cry harder if people forgot him. It brings me joy hearing people talking about my son."

I've found that over time, I've been able to let go of the grief and think of Code with happy thoughts. At first, I had so much guilt about his death. Why had I not known about his back getting worse? The last time he had come to visit us, he had mentioned that he'd had trouble breathing. I had told him if his back got any worse or if he found that he continued to have trouble breathing, he should get to the doctor.

He just replied, "Oh, Mom, I will survive." But I should have known he wouldn't go on his own. I just didn't realize how bad it was. I had to forgive myself for not knowing or I was going to go crazy.

I had so many regrets from not doing more as a family or not saying more than I did. I just thought I had lots of time. You never think your child will go before you. I used to think death came to the oldest first and worked its way down. Now, I realize death can come at any time and anywhere.

That is one of the reasons why this book is so important. I want to urge you not to leave doing things for later because "later" might never come. And don't leave things unsaid. If you have something to say, say it. We always think death won't happen to us or to our loved ones, but let me tell you, it will. I would never have thought we would be dealing with this but we are. You think something like this only happens to other families, not yours. You wish you could wake up and have things the way that they used to be, but you can't.

The one thing that gets me through is the knowledge that I will see Code again. And it helps to know that he is without pain and he is happy. I don't know how people can go on after something like this if they don't believe in an afterlife. It must be even more painful thinking they will never see their loved ones again. I hope that this book might open their eyes to believing that they *will* see them again, and that it will bring comfort. If I can do that, it would make me happy.

Maybe that's my mission in life. All of us like to think we have a purpose; maybe this book is mine.

Messages and Assistance from Heaven

At one point, Kalie told me, "I don't think I could love someone as much as I loved Seige." (which was her nickname for Cody.) Her partner, Greig, was trying to help her deal with losing her brother. This is how we ended up meeting Shelley. One of his co-workers had told him about her. Greig called her, and gave her a full interview to make sure she was the right person to help Kalie.

When Kalie went to see Shelley, she did not know what to expect from the meeting. Afterward, she called her dad and me on FaceTime, excited to tell us about her experience. Kalie told us that Shelley had been able to communicate with Code and he told her of all the signs he was sending to let us know that he was with us, and trying to comfort us.

I exclaimed to Kalie that I, too, had been getting different messages and to this, Kerry commented, "Well, I'm not getting any messages."

At that very moment, our home phone started to ring, but we were sitting on the couch away from the phone and talking to Kalie on our iPad. We thought we would just let the answering machine pick up the message but we were still listening to see who it was. The machine came on and there was just silence for a minute or two before it went off.

We finished our visit with Kalie and I went to the answering machine and checked the Caller ID. I was amazed to see our home phone number displayed. The phone had begun ringing right when Kerry had commented that he wasn't getting any of Code's messages. I took it to Kerry, showing him the Caller ID and said, "Here is your sign from Code. He just called you from Heaven."

Just to be sure, we tried everything possible to call ourselves so that our home number would appear but of course it can't be done. I took a picture of the phone with our number on the display to show people. We know without a doubt that it was Code letting his dad know that he is with him, too.

Our loved ones don't want us to be sad when they pass on but they understand that that's how we feel. They try to give us comfort whenever they see us having a hard time dealing with our grief. They send us subtle messages that will make us think of them with happy thoughts. They will give us different signs to let us know they are with us.

And for families left behind to miss them, they receive messages through the wind, stars, and rainbows. We will feel our loved ones through the elements, through air, water, and electronics.

That reminds me of a time I was having lunch with a good friend, Milada, in town. In the restaurant, they have hanging lights. Just behind where Milada was sitting, there was one light that I could see clearly from my point of view. When I started talking about Code, the light right behind her started to swing. When we talked about something else it would stop, and then when we talked about Code again it would start swinging.

About the third time, I started to laugh and Milada asked, "What's so funny?" I told her that Code was there. I asked her to turn around. "Oh, my God, you're right!" she exclaimed. It continued to happen every time we talked about him.

He also uses the wind to let us know he is present. After doing dishes one night, I walked over to his picture and started to talk to him. The star that hangs right by his picture started swinging and there was a "ping" out of the oil diffuser. I know it was Code; I could feel his presence.

Sometimes we can even smell odours associated with our loved ones, such as their perfume, their cigars, or their aftershave.

During a meeting with Shelley, one of the signs Code said to watch for was the colour purple and that if I saw it standing out, it would be because he has brought it to my attention as a sign that he is with me. One day, I went for a walk down by Lake Dorothy. I was missing Code and was talking to him just to feel that connection.

As I stood there looking out over the lake, admittedly somewhat tearfully, suddenly right in front of me, I noticed a bush with two purple flowers. There were no other bushes with flowers; they were all bare. Had I walked any further in either direction, there would have been no flowers to see. But there they were, two purple flowers, one for Code and one for me. I knew it was my son saying that he was still with me. That moment was so special.

Code explained to us that all of the major challenges in your life provide lessons for you to learn. He added that when you die, you review your life and learn from it.

Shelley explained that Code really hadn't wanted to be born. Then I remembered the hard birth he'd had, and the problems with his back. But he was meant to be here, at least for a while.

He said that we have six opportunities in life when our souls can decide to stay or to go. Through Shelly, I learned that Code could have died at a later age but the time that he did pass away was the best time for him. He was able to do more good by going early than he could have accomplished by staying.

He said that from the spirit world, you are able to see lifelines for others still on Earth. You cannot prevent events from happening to them but you can change the outcome.

Shelley mentioned that Code is able to guide us, just as his grandfather, Art, in spirit had been able to help him through his life. Art had passed away when Code was three weeks old. Shelley explained that Art would come and visit Code, watching him in his crib.

Through Shelley, Code told us that Art had saved our son's life on at least one occasion. One day when Code and his friend, Adam, were eleven years old, they went bike-riding down what we called Snake Hill in Windermere. This is a steep and winding road. Going as fast as they could, Code didn't see a hydro wire holding up a power pole, and he hit the line right across his neck, throwing him off his bike. Code told us that this would have killed him had it not been for Art, who was able to change the outcome of that event. We were always amazed that Code was able to walk away from this accident. Now we know why.

Our family is keeping Code busy. Explaining through Shelley, Code said that he has been able to do more good in heaven since he passed than he could have hoped to do during his life. He has been able to save so many of our family members and friends. They would have had different outcomes had it not been for Code.

First, Code's Uncle Bruce, my younger brother, was in Stanley Park on a bike trail just finishing his morning ride when a tour bus hit him from behind. The impact sent him and his bike flying through the air and into the ditch. He was seriously hurt but was able to make a full recovery. The firemen and ambulance drivers said that if Bruce had been hit just an inch this way or that, the bus would have gone right over top of him and would have crushed him. As Code explained through Shelley, he was able to make changes to the incident but couldn't stop it from happening.

Our nephew, Ken, was riding his motorbike on the Deerfoot Trail in Calgary. This is one of the busiest and fastest roads in the city. He had to stop for an accident and was hit from behind by a young adult who was texting on his phone while going full highway speed. Ken was thrown over two lanes of highway but received only minor damage and no broken bones. Ken, a fireman, was told by his co-workers that the only way anyone leaves the Deerfoot after being hit on a motorcycle at highway speed is in a body bag. Again, Code explained through Shelley that this accident would have had a different outcome had it not been for him.

Our niece, Christy, left her two young sons with her mom to do some errands. She was at an intersection when she was hit from behind, and she was injured. She was told that she was lucky that her sons were not in the back seat as the car was badly damaged.

Our nephew, Brad, was T-boned by another car while out in his vehicle. He was also injured but made a full recovery.

Code's best friend, Zack, was driving home from work. While trying to get something out of the back seat of his pickup truck, driving with his knees on the steering wheel at highway speed, his knee slipped and cut the wheel. The truck went up on two wheels and was ready to flip. Somehow, the vehicle came out of it. We received a phone call from Zack just after this happened. He was screaming and saying, "I know it was Code! He saved me. There is no way I could have got out of this. I had nowhere to go. I was dead, only Code saved me, I just know it!"

I remember driving one snowy night when the roads were icy. Just before the overpass heading into Invermere, I questioned, "Is that black ice?"

Before I knew it, I had lost control of my vehicle. I went completely sideways in the other lane. Coming down the hill toward me was a loaded semi-truck. It was going to hit me on the driver's side so I floored the gas and shot across the road. The snow caught my vehicle and spun it back toward the road, where I missed the semi but hit the flat deck of a truck behind it.

There was a metal box underneath the truck, which is what I hit. I'm sure that without it, I would have gone under the vehicle.

I was shaken up but otherwise all right. It could have been so much worse. I totalled my car but I was able to walk away with just a sore neck. I had nightmares for a week. I kept seeing that semi coming at me. I think my boy was watching over me.

Code has said that he is only able to help each person a few times, and then we are on our own. In the meantime, it is comforting to know that he is our special angel watching over us. He is really in his element. And like all spirits, he can be in more than one place at a time. He can be with Dad and me but also be watching over Kalie.

Different Vibrations

The last time that I went to see Shelley, Code told me that he had graduated in the spirit world and was in a school of a different kind. He explained that there are different light levels. We are all vibrational beings, giving off vibrational signals. This is why you feel comfortable with some people when you first meet them. Your vibrations are at the same frequency as theirs. When you feel uncomfortable or it's difficult to be around others, your frequencies do not match. Different vibrations give off different light.

Code explained that his light had gotten dimmer the last three years of his life. He had dimmed his light to be at the same level as the people with whom he was spending his time.

Because of the work he had done since he passed, his light had changed to more purple and white with a touch of pink. He had been able to graduate and now he has a beautiful sphere.

During one appointment with Shelley, I learned that both Kerry and I had been instrumental in elevating

Code as a soul. Kerry had been thinking he had let Code down as a father, and that maybe he had been too hard on him. Because of his regrets and negative thoughts on this subject, Kerry had been experiencing one ailment after another. But Code had a strong message for his father.

"Dad's love for me helped me through my struggles in life." Code explained that prior to his passing, he had been in the grey and about to go into the blackness but he could see his Dad's face and the love Code didn't have for himself. Because of that, our son was able to come into the light and turn his life around.

"Tell him that he was the best Dad ever. I love you Dad. I love you, and you saved me. You did what you were supposed to do and gave me tough love at times when I needed it, as Mom was unable to do. Dad, your love, and Mom always believing in me were both important."

Hearing Code's message of love and gratitude for his father saved Kerry, just as much as Kerry had saved Code. Men are human, too, and they can have moments of brokenness also. I think that they feel they have to be strong and not show emotion. This can be so unhealthy. A friend of mine told me that her husband tried to ignore the loss of their son. It took three years for the loss to sink in and then he had a nervous breakdown.

Ignoring the loss just doesn't work. The sooner you do acknowledge it, the better you can deal with it. Talking and sharing with other survivors of this kind of loss helps so much.

For some people, religious or spiritual beliefs are another important factor when grieving a tremendous loss. One day when I was missing Code, I picked up my Bible in search of comfort. It opened to this passage: "For though I am absent from you in body, I am present with you in spirit and delight to see how orderly you are and how firm your faith in Christ is." I found great comfort in these words, especially knowing what Code had said through Shelley about being with me and with others who miss him.

He told us to love his soul but let go of his ashes, which I still had at home. One comment Code made was, "Mom, what do you do with an old vehicle?" This helped me to realize that I was holding onto him in a way that was not good for either of us. I understood that his spirit is still with us and that he is no longer a part of the ashes, nor is he connected to them in any way.

Finally, it was time to let them go so I wouldn't hold him back by clinging to a physical representation of him.

Nor did I want to hold him back by needing him to stay close and allow me to feel his presence. It had been a journey to get to that point but I could finally recognize that to do that to his soul would be selfish of me. If he needed to raise his vibration to further evolve as a soul, we might not feel him with us any longer but I knew we would be fine.

Code also told us that we were to get another dog, a border collie. He explained that the dog would be able to see him, and would bark to let us know that he is with us. We would see how happy he is through the dog's energy. Code mentioned that he now has more energy than he did here on Earth. This would be because as a soul, his vibrational frequency has increased beyond what humans are capable of achieving.

Code wanted me to write this book to help people deal with losing a loved one, and it can also help those in the spirit world. Sometimes they are stuck at the same level and can't elevate themselves if the vibrations of their loved ones on Earth are angry or bitter and won't let them go. It might be that they are angry with their loved ones for dying, and they won't forgive them. Sometimes it's because of the state in which their loved ones have left them, like with debt or other unfinished business.

Code stated there are so many of these souls at this level that they are backlogged. Those of us left here on Earth need to release any painful feelings tied to our loved ones in spirit. We must forgive them and resolve any conflict. Otherwise, they will be trapped at the same level until we die and can then deal with the conflict and resolve the issues.

In getting this message out to the world, Code is a light from the other side. He is lifting the veil, and people will be drawn to this book to help elevate and release the backlog of souls that are stuck in this conflict.

Comforting Visits

It might sound odd, but after Code passed, Kalie and I always cleared the seat in the car so he would have a place to sit. Through Shelley, he just laughed and said, "You don't need to do this!"

I had thought Code would like his music more than mine when we were driving so I always played it. But he laughed again. "Mom, stop listening to my music!"

Shelley told me that he wanted us to take lots of pictures at family gatherings. He said we were to look for "orbs" in the photos and this is how we would be able to "see him."

I know Code has been with us ever since his passing. I have been able to feel him sit beside me at night. In those earliest dark times, although he understood that I needed to experience the pain before I could begin to heal he would say, "Mom you're not supposed to cry. You're supposed to celebrate."

Shelley had explained that one of the ways our loved ones communicate with us is through our dreams. This is because when we're dreaming, we are completely open and receptive to connecting with their spirits. Our barriers are gone. So when dreams of loved ones are particularly vivid, those aren't dreams; they are actually visits.

I have had some vivid dreams that were visits from Code. The first was shortly after losing him. It had been so real. In the dream, Code and I were down in the basement of our old house in Windermere. He would have been about five or six years old. He wrapped his arms around my neck. "Mom, we have the best family! I love you so much!"

This made me so happy!

The second dream was a few months later. I dreamed Code was standing nearby and when I saw him I called, "Cody! I've missed you so much!" I hugged him and again it was so real I can still feel him. In the dream, I asked him what I could cook for him and started listing all of his favourite things to eat. He gave me that beautiful "Cody look" and then I woke up. It was a bittersweet moment; I was happy that I got to experience how it felt to hug him again and to see him, but sad because I wanted him to stay with me longer.

In another dream, he and I were sitting together outside sharing a smoke, just talking and visiting with each other like we had done so often before he passed. I was always honoured that he felt comfortable in opening up to me the way he would do. The dream was just as vivid as if he had actually been here. It had felt so good to be with him again and I woke up happy.

Dreams of our loved ones can bring so much comfort but we are not to try and force them. Sadness keeps us from experiencing them more often. Just let the dreams come naturally. This is the best way to be able to have them and to remember them.

I can feel him at times and I will say, "Code, is that you?" It has been so healing to know that until the day we are together again he will always be nearby, even if there comes a time when I can no longer feel his presence.

Often, he lifts my spirits when I feel down by sending me signs that he is here. I just have to keep an open mind and be aware. I know there are some people who are unable to sense their loved ones being close but it doesn't mean they aren't there.

Because I could feel Code's presence quite frequently, through Shelley I asked him if I was holding him back from doing whatever else he was supposed to be doing and he said, no, he is where he should be, which is with us to help us through this hard time. He replied, "Mom, you are my sun, moon and stars. You are my everything." I don't think Code could have given me a better compliment than this.

He went on to say that he would be with me until we are together again, adding, "I will be the first one you see when you pass to this side." It gives me great comfort to know he is waiting for me. But he did say, "First you have some living to do, Mom!"

He is right. Although I would love to see him again, I know that our time here on Earth will pass in the blink of an eye and Code says it is insignificant compared to that which is to come. There is so much more for us after death that we cannot imagine it. Life here on Earth is such a small part of everything. Code said it is awesome there. I think this will give people so much comfort knowing there is life after death, and that it is more magnificent than we could ever imagine.

I am grateful for the time I was given with my son. Many families are not as fortunate to have as much time with their loved ones as I had with him. Some lose their children at birth, in early childhood or in their teens.

And I am also grateful for the way that Code died. I was told by the coroner that he would have felt no pain, and that he had simply gone to sleep and awakened in heaven. I'm glad for this, as parents do not want their children to suffer.

I remember quite some time ago watching the Oprah Winfrey show on TV. The program was about people who have been killed in car crashes while on their cell phones. One story in particular really stands out in my mind. It was a father so heartbroken. He blamed himself for his son's death. The father had called his son on his cell phone and the son answered the call, taking his eyes off the road and hitting a tree. The poor man was so full of grief; it was utterly heartbreaking.

This happened probably thirty years ago and I'm still thinking of him. I know grief can make you sick if you let it, and I have always wondered what became of him. If I could ever find him, I would love to share with him the good news that our loved ones are alive in spirit. Based on what Code has said, there is no doubt that the young man's spirit has been trying to show his father signs that his son is still with him. I hope the father has been able to see them.

I feel sorry for people who don't believe that our souls live on. How they must fear death. How hopeless they must feel when they lose someone they love. I get excited thinking that one day I will see Code again and be reunited with him. In the meantime, I still have a beautiful life with my daughter, Kalie, and my husband, Kerry and I value it more than I can say. We are not to focus on when we will be with Cody again and instead, we are meant to live full and happy lives.

Our First Christmas

As is to be expected, our first Christmas without Code was so painful. There was a huge hole in it where he used to be.

Code loved Christmas and everything about it. He would get so excited to open gifts. He would sit and look at the presents for days. The rule at our house was to wait till the four of us were up before any gifts were opened.

I remember the smile on Code's face when he opened his last gift. He had asked for slippers for Christmas, which we had got him, but I had also noticed that his boots were quite well worn and he needed new ones.

Just when he thought he had opened all of his gifts, I said, "Code, you have one more." I'll never forget the look on his face when he opened it to find a new pair of his beloved Timberlands boots.

One of my most treasured memories of our last Christmas together is with Kerry, Kalie, Code and me sitting in our hot tub. The snow was falling lightly and all of us were drinking Caesars. I remember telling them that this was all I ever wanted for Christmas, for the four of us to be together and that it was the best gift of all.

How true those words came to be. I will always remember that special Christmas with so much love.

The next year, our first without Code, Kalie spent Christmas Eve with her partner Grieg's parents, so it was just going to be Kerry and me for gift-opening in the morning. When he and I got up on Christmas Day, we looked where Code always sat to open his gifts and we burst into tears. The void was so strong, it was a good thing Kalie was not there to see us so heartbroken.

By the time she arrived, Kerry and I knew we had to be strong for her, to make the most of Christmas and be cheerful for her sake. The last gift I gave to Kalie was a pillow made out of Code's favourite shirts. I had pictures of all of us on it, along with some of Code's favourite sayings, like "Loves ya, Kay," and "I'm not lucky, I'm blessed." I had made pockets on the pillow and put Code's lip balm, lighter and one of his favourite pocketknives inside them. Inside the last pocket we had a beautiful thumb print necklace made for Kalie. We had an imprint of Code's thumb, which included a callous. We added Code's birthstone, a ruby. Kalie has never taken the necklace off. She told me that she rubs it and when she feels Code's callous, this brings her comfort.

Kalie had a surprise for us, too. She had collected favourite memories of Code from family and friends and put together the most amazing book. I just couldn't believe how she was able to do all of this while going to university. Every time I look at this book, it fills me with many happy memories. It is such a treasure.

That first Christmas Day was very difficult, but with Kalie and Greig to help us through it, we did it. I told Kerry that I wanted to go away the next Christmas as it was just so hard without Code. Then I remembered how much Kalie loves Christmas, too, and it would be selfish of me to take this from her.

One thing I have to mention is that all through Christmas Day, we could feel Code's presence. We knew he was with us, and trying to help us. Every time we started to feel down, we could feel Code trying to boost our spirits.

It helped having others around and keeping myself busy. And I would think of Code saying, "Mom I'm right here, I'm not gone."

Knowing he is still nearby has helped us to get through Christmases since then, as well as every other day, whether a special occasion or not.

Messages From Code

In attempting to feel my son's presence, he had said, "Don't force it, just be patient." He said to keep my eyes downward and he will come. One night, I was sitting on the couch just listening for his insight on life. First, it was like a vivid motion picture soaring over the mountains in 3D. I felt like an eagle. I think what he was trying to get across to me was that there is a big, beautiful world out there. We are such a small part of it. There is more than this world in the grand scheme of things.

He wants me to say that we are not to let this life get us down. In the end, we will realize that most of what we dealt with is really not important; let it go and don't let it define you. Our time here will pass quickly; don't waste it on unhappiness. Try every day to find something that brings you happiness, whether it's a person, or doing something you enjoy. When you are happy, this rubs off on others around you.

Another strong message I was getting from Code is to love one another, and to be kind and accepting. Forgive one another, let go of the past and the wrongs. Get rid of hatred and judgement. Think of others before yourself.

I can only imagine what a wonderful world it would be if all of us followed these principles. I think Code is trying to share a little bit of heaven. It can start with one person who would pass it onto another and so on. Everyone wants to be accepted and to be loved; people are hungry for it.

Believing in an afterlife brings peace. You know where you are going when you pass away and you have nothing to fear. You look forward to seeing your loved ones who are in spirit. And although in the meantime you miss the physical connection such as hugging them, or hearing their laughter, you know that they are always with you.

We may go through trials and hardships, but as Code explained, our time here on Earth is such a small piece of the big picture. There is so much more, it would blow our minds to know what is coming.

Don't shut the door on the rest of the world. By this, I mean don't become a recluse. Keep in contact with friends, especially the ones who let you talk about your loss.

Try to stay active. It would be so easy to find relief from a bottle but try to limit yourself. With booze, you feel up while you're drinking but when you stop, boy, do you feel down. Alcohol is a depressant and can make you sadder so be careful.

Fresh air helps. Take lots of walks. My daughter, Kalie, gave me a blank book and asked me to write in it every day about anything for which I am thankful. I looked at it at the time, thinking, "What do I have to be thankful for? I've lost my son."

Then I looked at what was in front of me, my daughter Kalie. I looked over at my husband, Kerry, and said to myself, "Yes, I still have so very much to be thankful for. I just needed to be reminded. Thanks, Sweetie."

On the anniversary of the day Code passed away, Kalie went hiking up to the Tea Hut at Lake Louise. Unbeknown to Kalie, the weather was really cold and snowy on the top of the mountain. She was wearing capri pants, thinking, "This is June!"

When she got to the top, she took out a picture of Code along with his cross, and had a spicy Caesar in his honour. Kalie was so cold. The sky was grey, half raining and half snowing. She said, "Seige, if you are with me, send me a sign."

She told us that out of the grey sky came an opening in the clouds and a ray of sunshine shone directly on her. There was no sun anywhere else, just on her.

She started to laugh and cry as that was the best sign of all. She remarked that it was like having a big Cody hug that warmed her right up. "Seige, you are the best, always letting us know you are with us," she said.

A couple of days later, I went to bed missing my boy so very much. As I was lying in bed, the dresser mirror started glowing, yet I had no light on in the bedroom. I knew it was Code letting me know he was with me, and he was trying to bring comfort. He is so giving and is always trying to let us know he is with us.

Kerry and I went camping at Premier Lake, our favourite place to go camping. We have so many great memories of time spent there with Kalie and Code. When I think of that place, it makes me smile.

It was Saturday night. Kerry and I were sitting around the campfire along with good friends of ours, Rod and Johanna. We were telling them some of the stories from previous camping trips there. We all looked up at the sky and it was like stars were coming right at us. I exclaimed, "Look, Kerry!"

At that very moment, a shooting star went one direction and just to let us know it was Code and to make sure we didn't miss it, another shooting star went in the other direction. I think he was enjoying us telling stories of our camping trips and the good times we had, and he wanted to let us know he was with us.

Code was always really protective of me. I remember once when I went to visit him in Blackfalds, there was an ice storm. We came out of his trailer and ice was covering everything. It was so icy, my girlfriend and I could hardly stand up. Code yelled at his friend Zack to come and help walk us to our hotel. I remember him saying, "Hold on tight, Mom, I won't let you fall." We were both laughing and sliding. It was another great memory for us to cherish, and a reminder of how important it is to take care of each other.

Now I have Code as my guardian angel. When I start to fear something or I'm unsure of what to do, I just trust in him. I also trust in God. I always talk to both.

My daughter, Kalie, was telling me that she also prays to both. I'm sure the Lord would be okay with this.

One night, Kerry and I were in our hot tub. We were thinking of Code and right then I looked up and there in the sky was a perfect "C." The whole sky was dark but this "C" was bright white. I know it was Code letting us know once again that he was with us.

I remember another visit from him. I was dreaming about talking to a hockey coach and then beside me was Code. Kerry and I both had colds and sore throats and it sounded like Code had one also.

In the dream, he asked if I had the keys for Code Red so he could go for a rip in it! I said, "Sure, but I need a hug first!" Code gave me the biggest hug, I rubbed his whiskers and then I woke up, the feeling of that beautiful, warm hug still fresh in my mind.

On a different night, I had such a wonderful dream about Code. I dreamed we were back in Windermere School, a place with great memories. We were sitting beside each other in a classroom. I was holding Code's hand, discussing movies and which ones we wanted to see, something we used to loved to do.

Just then, two men walked into the classroom, Code knew that I needed to touch him and he wasn't embarrassed having his mom holding his hand. He was proud of it. We just kept talking and visiting; it was so comforting. When I woke up, I was so uplifted.

Because of our loss, Code is also indirectly responsible for other messages that are important for me to share. You don't have to spend a lot of money to show your kids that you love them. You don't have to go on big holidays and have fancy material things. All your kids want is to spend time with you and to receive love from you.

I have so many memories of good times with Kalie and Code. One time, we went camping in my Mom and Dad's trailer at Premier Lake, our favourite place. The trailer had no power or plumbing but we had a roof over our heads. Good thing, because it started raining hard.

We brought the kids into the trailer out of the rain and put a fuzzy fleece blanket on the bed. We played the game, *"Trouble,"* ate chips and had the best time. This is one of my favourite memories of camping…just being together.

One of the most important messages I want to share as a result of our tragic loss is how essential it is to make time for your kids. Drop whatever you are doing if they need you or need a hug; you don't always get a second chance. Love them and never, ever give up on them. If you always believe in them, it will help them to believe in themselves.

And there's nothing more important than loving them unconditionally. Love them when they make mistakes or if they do something wrong. Code said our unconditional love had been instrumental in helping to elevate his soul.

Always let people know how you feel; don't be afraid to say, "I love you." Never pass an opportunity to let someone know you care.

The Time of Your Life

When Kerry and I were in Mexico a while after losing Code, one night I was having a hard time with my grief. I went up to the bedroom and out onto the balcony. I asked Code if he was there. I said that I just missed him so much. It was a clear, moonlit night.

In the sky was a white dot that started to get bigger and bigger. No clouds had blown in; the dot just appeared all by itself in the middle of the sky. It was truly comforting. I whispered, "Code, you are amazing. Thanks so much for letting us know you are here! You are so special."

On another night, I was having a tough time thinking of Mother's Day coming up. I couldn't have the only thing I wanted. I just missed Code so much and started to cry, as did Kerry.

A few minutes later, we both looked up into the sky. The cloud formation looked just like Code's ribs, and his back with the curve. Both Kerry and I noticed at the same time.

"Gee, those clouds look just like Code's back," I commented. "He is letting us know he is in a better place and has no pain." Such a peace came over us. Thanks for that message, Code!

Kerry and I went to Palm Springs for another holiday. One night, I woke up wondering where Kerry was. I walked out onto the balcony and could hear that he was upset. I put my arms around him, trying to comfort him and he broke down. He was recalling a time when we had been getting ready to go camping. He had been all worked up and wanted to get away. I didn't want to leave until Code arrived from Sylvan Lake. Finally, Code walked into the house but Kerry said, "Okay, now let's go," and didn't hug Code goodbye. Kerry had not forgiven himself for that.

"I missed that hug!" he cried on that Palm Springs balcony. "If I could just have another chance!"

As we stood there, we were both looking out into the night when over our heads there appeared a fireball. This was not an ordinary falling star; this one was like a meteorite. It shot over our heads and neither Kerry nor I could believe our eyes. A powerful sense of peace came over us.

I remember Kalie telling me that one night she was coming home from school, missing Code. She had moved her books off the front seat of the car. "I miss you, Seige, please come for a ride," she had whispered.

Once she got home, she sat in the car in the driveway and cried. She looked out her rear-view mirror and noticed the streetlights had started to blink off and on.

Just then, the popular band Green Day came on the radio, singing their lyrics, "*I hope you had the time of your life.*"

Kalie started to laugh and cry at the same time, feeling Code's presence. "Way to go, Seige, I know you are here!"

Later, she told me, "You just know Code is with you, you can feel him, and like that song says, '*Sometimes it's unpredictable but in the end it's right, I hope you had the time of your life.*'"

Code you are amazing. You are always comforting us and letting us know you are here. We love you so very much.

Code's Bench

Everyone wanted to do something in memory of Code. With the help of family and friends, we had the most beautiful bench made. It sits up on a hill above the valley. This was one of Code's favourite places to park and admire the amazing view. Through Shelley, he told us that he would meet us on the hill, and that he loves the bench.

We are so glad to have that bench. Sometime before he passed, Code and his friend, Zack, had a tree. Where they got it, I don't know but it was already in a pot and ready to be planted. The boys had left it with "Mama Julie," Zack's mom, who then gave the tree to us. It turned out that Kerry had been watering this tree for months and wondering why.

The funny thing is that then one day, through Shelley Code asked us to plant a tree for him by the bench. In fact, the tree had always reminded Kerry and me of Code's back because it has a curve in it.

Code wanted us to have a party on the anniversary of the day he passed. As was previously mentioned, this was because being born into heaven was like a birthday.

Through Shelley, Code even gave Kalie the menu he wanted for the party, which contained all of his favourite food.

I asked all of his and Kalie's friends, plus our friends and family to join in the celebration. We decided that this would be the perfect time to dedicate Code's bench to him and we would plant the tree on that occasion.

The weekend before the dedication, we had to prepare the ground for the bench. First, we had to make it level. We had a friend, Dave Fuller, come with his little backhoe to do the job. He was able to prepare a spot for the bench, as well as a place for a flower garden.

The next day another friend, Guy Fournier came to help with the concrete. Kerry brought Max Helmer Construction's concrete truck and we poured the pad for the bench. While Kerry was taking the truck back to wash it out, Guy asked me where Code's ashes were. I told him I had them at the house. It was before I'd found it in myself to let them go.

Guy and I went to the house, where he helped me to open the box and remove some of Code's ashes to spread into the concrete. I cannot tell you what a feeling it is to have your son's ashes in your hands. No words can say how truly broken I felt. Thank goodness for Shelley because at that moment, I remembered her sharing that message from Code months earlier. "Be happy for me,

Mom. I'm in such a good place, it's awesome, and I have no pain; it's the best video game ever."

Some time before the bench dedication, I had started cooking for the event plus everyone brought food. I had also jokingly asked Code for help with the weather. "I'm going to need sunshine! Well, at least not rain because I don't know what I'm going to do with everyone in our house and all this food!"

Later, as we were walking up to the bench, cars were going by and they were covered in hail. The town of Invermere had been hit by a wicked hailstorm. When we were all up at the bench and we could see how black it was in town but the sun came out and shone on us. It felt like Code was watching over us.

It was a very special day. We got some great pictures and a few of the girls planted flowers. Then everyone came back to the farm for a barbecue. It was such a blessing having so many of our friends and family members joining us for the celebration.

On July 6, 2016 I woke up at 2:17 a.m., the very time Code was born 23 years earlier. I can still remember what a hard time Code had coming into this world, but what joy he had brought us. He was such a beautiful baby. Even my Dad commented, "Well, he's not ugly, he's beautiful!"

I laughed, "What did you expect?" and he responded, "Marj, newborns are not beautiful but he is."

I thought of these and other memories as I was looking at Code's picture. I couldn't help but wish him a happy birthday.

The previous evening, Kerry had come home in tears. He had missed getting to the Dollar Store before it closed. He had wanted to get balloons in honour of Code's birthday. So the next morning, I went right away to get them. I took them down to where Kerry works and tied one to his truck to let him know that I had got them.

I went up to the bench and tied some balloons on it and then tied some on Code Red. I made Code's favourite meal for supper: steak, potatoes, and corn on the cob. After supper, Kerry and I went up to the bench to have a drink and to reminisce about our son's birth. And on remembering Code saying for us to look for him in "orbs" in photographs, we took some pictures.

When we were up there, we were looking for signs from him and we got a beautiful rainbow.

On another day, Kerry and I had spent the day working around the farm. We decided it was time to take Code Red for a spin. We had been parking the truck just below the house to remind everyone of Code and all the good times they shared with him. We asked people to honk their horns when they drove by.

Kerry smiled, "Let's go for a ride up to Code's bench!"

We hopped in and had the music cranked right up. As we were heading off to the bench, the song "Renegade" came on the radio. This song has always reminded us of a favourite memory of Code. On one of our trips to see him at Sylvan Lake, we had picked him up and were driving downtown. This song had come on the radio and all three of us had sung along with smiles on our faces.

As Kerry and I drove up to his bench with this song bringing back sweet memories, he and I hollered, "Yahoo!" We knew Code was riding along with us. It was so very special

Through Shelley, Code told us that he is at the bench with anyone who goes there. I love spending time there; I feel close to him again and it brings me peace. I always feel better afterwards.

I remember one particular day that had begun with a rough start. I hadn't slept well and was tired. Knowing that I would feel better after a visit to the bench, I hopped on my bike and away I went. I sat and thought about many happy memories of my son.

All of a sudden, a sunbeam shone on me and I felt its warmth. It was like getting a Cody hug. Suddenly, I remembered Kalie telling me about that day she had gone hiking up at the Tea Hut in Banff when it had been so cold and she, too, had experienced a warm ray of sunshine that was just on her and nowhere else.

Code is so good at sending signs that he is with us and we are grateful to be aware of them.

Forgive Yourself

On another occasion when Kalie and I went to see Shelley, wow!! What a visit. I was able to get messages from Code again; this was so healing. Code told me that he loves being with me, but his biggest message was, "Mom, forgive, forgive, forgive yourself." Code knew I was having trouble with that and I know other parents who have lost their sons and daughters need to hear this also, that losing our children does not mean we were failures as parents. We have to forgive ourselves and know we did the best that we could.

One of the toughest things for which I had to forgive myself was not giving Code a cross that had been bought to replace one that he had lost. Initially, Kerry and I had given him one from a trip to Mexico. It was Code's pride and joy. He thought of it as being in celebration of getting through all the hard times of the past and it was also a reminder of how far he had come.

Code was at work at NTL and was roughhousing with one of the guys when he lost his cross accidentally.

I remember him coming back home broken-hearted about it. His Uncles Rick and Paul were going to Mexico and I had asked them if they could pick up another cross to replace the one that Code had lost.

What a beautiful cross they got for him! I was going to give it to Code when a friend of mine advised me to give it to Code for his birthday. A few weeks before that special date, Code had come back home. We were sitting on his bed talking about his cross. It would have been the perfect time to give him the replacement cross but I thought how special it would be for his birthday.

Code passed away just after that day and I never got to give the cross to him. I never got to see his joy in receiving it. How I wished I had given him this gift! I never dreamed that he would not be here for his birthday just three weeks later.

Code's message about forgiving myself was one of the most healing of all the messages he had shared. I did my best to do as he had instructed. Now I wear his cross with pride and feel him close.

I also had to forgive myself for not making Code go to the doctor the last time he was down for a visit. I felt like a true failure as a mom. Mothers are supposed to know these things. We are the ones who are to direct our children and what actions to take. I couldn't help but feel like I should have made Code go to the doctor. Sometimes I wondered if maybe I would have still had my son had I done this.

But then I remember him saying that his soul had chosen to leave when it did. I remember everything he had said about that through Shelley. Our souls choose the time that they leave this life and there was nothing I could have done to prevent it being his time to go.

This allowed me to let go of any guilt I'd been feeling about being responsible for my son's death. I had always done my best for him and there was no way I could have known what was to come. It was time to forgive myself and move forward.

Healing After Loss

Knowing Code is not gone and that his spirit is still nearby has been so healing for Kalie, Kerry and me. At times when I felt like I couldn't make it, he has sent me a sign to say he was still close. It is so sad to think that many people who are grieving don't see the signs that their loved ones have been sending. They are not paying attention, or if they see something that reminds them of their loved ones, they think it's coincidence or their imagination.

It was Thanksgiving, our second one without Cody. I had a dream that we were back at our old trailer. It was similar to the one Kerry and I lived in before we were married. In the dream, I walked in and the first thing I saw was our cat, Bagheera, and Code was sitting there playing with him. He loved animals of any kind; it didn't matter.

I asked him for a hug. He stood up and did as I had requested. While he was hugging me, he was playing with the cat on the side and I joked, "Stop playing with the cat and give me a big hug!"

He smiled, "It's okay, Mom, I'm right here." I could still feel that Cody hug when I woke up. What a special Thanksgiving present.

I have to tell you a story about the first time Code came home and saw Bagheera. He was a rescue cat and he had been getting into a lot of fights. Because of that, he was pretty banged up. He had stitches and as he had been shaved, he was missing some hair.

Code walked into the house and I pointed. "This is our new cat."

Code replied, "Wow, talk about your fixer-upper!"

Before long, I found the two of them curled up together on the couch asleep.

Animals know when spirits are here with us. I'm sure Bagheera can see Code when he appears to be looking at something but we can't see anything. As mentioned earlier, this is one of the reasons Code wants us to get another dog because it will let us know when he is with us.

Code and Daisy, my sister's golden retriever, used to go for a walk just about every day. I know Daisy adored him so perhaps she can see him. She and Code would hunt for squirrels, which drove Code's Auntie Shirley crazy, as she liked the little animals but Code didn't want them around a fort that he and his friends had been building at the farm.

Each day, Kerry would bring home more wood and nails for this fort that just seemed to get bigger all the time. All of Code's friends enjoyed pounding nails out there. When it was finished, the fort was three stories high and had a bridge. It was quite the sight to see.

Code was so proud of that fort. He took me up one day to show me that he had added another floor and also had a big armchair that he had suspended with ropes. To be honest, I was a little nervous as we got to the second floor and we were going up to the third. He laughed, "Mom, look, it's safe!" and he started jumping up and down. Everything was shaking, and the whole time he just smiled.

One of the messages Code wanted me to share was that we don't need to stay sad to honour our loved ones in spirit. It's not like you will ever forget them. In fact, you're probably thinking of them a lot of the time, certainly in the earliest months after they pass.

You honour them by being happy and doing things that bring you joy. They celebrate this. They will always be with us. I think of Code a lot and as time has passed and I've been healing, now I'm happy talking about him and laughing as I recall some of our experiences.

We have so much love to give and when we lose our children, we still have that love inside us and we should give it to others. I remember growing up on the Upper Ranch and my Dad saying, "Kids keep you young." He was right. To have kids around did keep us young.

Therefore, after the initial challenges of dealing with losing Code, eventually it was time for us to get involved with life again. So Kerry and I took in international students. Code was so excited for us and knew that this would be good for us in many ways.

Kalie was happy with our decision to get the international students. She was busy with school; we knew that and we didn't want her worrying about us. Kerry and I thought getting students would be a positive experience. We would meet new people and rediscover our valley and all the things we had taken for granted.

Taking in a couple of students also helped to ease the transition from having Code and his friends around regularly, especially when I baked, something I love doing and find to be relaxing. Prior to his passing, Code, Kalie and their friends would walk into the house and say, "Wow, it smells so good in here!" I loved seeing the smiles on their faces as they enjoyed the baking and good meals.

I am comforted by the many beautiful memories of those precious times with my son and his friends. They light up my heart and make me smile.

Some people who have not lost anyone really close to them are uncomfortable talking about death. Usually, it's the ones who have had that experience who are more than willing to talk and compare notes. Those who believe in life after death know exactly what you're saying when you mention signs.

There are so many people out there with whom I want to share that good news. You can believe or not; it's totally up to you. But if you don't believe it, you might miss the signs that your loved ones are sending to comfort you. Maybe you could at least be open to the idea, be receptive to noticing or feeling their spirits.

Many people feel uncomfortable talking about death because they worry about how it will happen, or they wonder if they will have to suffer first. But whether or not we're uncomfortable with the idea, however it comes, it is going to happen to all of us someday.

Not talking about it will not prevent it and it won't prepare us for it either. It's almost as if some people think that by not talking about it, they will be immune to it. I have news for them. They're not.

I find it really interesting how people feel. I had a good friend ask me the other day how to prepare herself for death. She wasn't raised with any particular spiritual beliefs and didn't know where to start. She was really curious and asked me lots of questions. She enjoyed hearing about my experiences with Code, courtesy of Shelley, and how much it has helped us to know absolutely that our loved ones are still close after they return to the spirit world.

A lady came into the bank where I work not long after I'd heard that she had lost her daughter. I have known the woman for many years. She was trying to get her daughter's affairs in order. As I was helping her, I told her that I had lost Code and understood how she felt. She looked at me and started to cry. I told her, "One day at a time. It's like a rollercoaster, you're up, then you're down. But you *will* be up again."

I told her that I was still in disbelief at times as the truth is difficult to accept. But I wanted to share with her Code's message that he's with me, and to let her know that all you have to do is ask and your loved ones will show you signs to let you know they are with you.

We didn't have much time to talk but she told me that she had to remove all of her daughters' pictures and belongings at home because it was too hard to have them around. I told her that it was just the opposite for me; I have pictures of Code all over the house.

I had a photograph right there beside me at work and she asked if that was our family. "Yes," I replied, "those faces are what keep me going."

She thanked me, saying how much it had meant to her to be able to talk with someone who has gone through the loss of a child. I know it really helped me also, as no one can truly understand unless they have experienced it themselves.

As I have mentioned, I believe that part of my purpose in this life is to write this book and help others deal with their grief. Thanks to Shelley's help in getting Code's messages to us and in explaining many aspects of how all of this works, I've healed significantly and am able to pass along much of what I've learned.

I've learned that it is important to always let the negative feelings go, and to let go of all the regrets. If not, they can make you unhealthy, even deathly sick. Pray for comfort and strength, and God and your loved one in spirit will try to help you.

Through Shelley, Code has given me a lot of advice and helped me to understand things that he wanted me to share with you. He said to be open to change; after a significant loss you're not the same person you once were. A loss this great changes how you think and how you deal with life. It puts into perspective what's important and what is not. Like Code explained previously, many of our issues are "small stuff" and in the end will not be important.

Code's greatest message, though, is the reassurance of our loved ones being with us after they are in spirit.

When my mom passed away a while ago, some of the family had gathered together at my sister Shirley's house. I was saying that I could feel Code's spirit with me at times. Shirley had a funny look on her face and I asked her what was wrong. She explained that she didn't believe that Code's spirit was with us, and that she believed that he was in heaven.

Three months later, I had gone to see Shelley. She and I were getting to the end of our conversation when she said, "Code wants you to pass this message on to his Auntie Shirley: 'I am in heaven but I can come for visits, too.' Does this make any sense to you?"

I was blown away by this message! "Yes, this makes total sense to me!" I replied. Oh, how this made my day! The only way it could have been better is if Shirley had been there!

Angels on Earth

A friend of mine lost her husband. We had not been very close but we worked together and had gotten to know each other. We were at work when the news came regarding her husband.

From that moment, we bonded. She had a little girl and I would go over and visit the two of them. I remember her telling me that she had to get out of the house or she was going to go crazy. I would take them with me to go on road trips or to see other friends. We were together much of the time. I stayed with her a lot and helped her through that very difficult time.

Eventually, I was able to get her laughing and having fun again. It had felt like I was meant to do this and it felt so natural to help her when she needed me. Two years later, she met someone and moved away.

I'd had a similar experience of bonding with someone from work. I had hurt myself badly while skiing and was in hospital for three weeks. At this time, another girl had gotten sick at work and was on leave. Our boss had brought in a lady called Cindy to help while the two of us were off.

Cindy had come for a six-month contract. She ended up staying for five years. She became one of my dearest friends and got to know our family very well. She was having dinner with us when we received the news about Code. She was with me through some of the most difficult periods after that.

When I went back to work, she would watch me and if she saw that I was having trouble with my feelings, there she was. I cannot imagine how I would have gotten through that time in my life without her.

She got the news one day that she was being transferred. By that time, I was much stronger emotionally. I didn't need her in the same way as I had in those early days but I would miss the woman who had become my dear friend.

I think the good Lord puts people in our lives when we need them to help us deal with difficult events. I don't think anything happens by chance and certainly not those treasured meetings with Earth Angels.

My best friend from childhood, Louise, is another example. I sometimes wonder if she has ESP. I will be thinking about something and wonder how I'm going to deal with it and then the phone rings and it's Louise. She and I have stood up for each other when we got married and been there for each of our kids' births. Kalie and Code always called her Auntie Louise. She was the first person Kerry called when we got the news about Code.

I thank the good Lord every day for giving me a friend like this. Our dearest friends want to help us and if you're looking for comfort after the loss of a loved one, your close friends will want to be there for you to listen and support you. Don't be afraid to reach out to them.

I remember Louise saying to me, "Whenever you need to talk about Code, I'm here any time." It was nice to hear her say this. I didn't have to feel like I should just "get over it." True friends are our special angels on earth.

I don't know why some prayers are answered "Yes," and others are answered, "No." Maybe one day we will understand. My faith in God has helped me to accept the loss of my son and to trust that there must be a reason for it, even if I don't know what the reason is. And of course, now I know without a doubt that I will see my son again and this has helped so much, too.

Please know that your loved ones are with you and are trying to bring you comfort. You have only to pay attention and watch for the signs. You might question things that have happened and think, "This can't be!" But yes, it can. I hope that by sharing my story and experiences, you will be comforted.

I will never forget my son. Certain songs, smells or other triggers continue to bring back memories but now I can talk about Code with a smile. It is all a healing process, a journey. You might feel like you will never get through it, but just focus on one day at a time and you will learn to live with your loss.

Death is not the end but rather, it is the beginning of something beautiful. There is peace in knowing that someday we will see our loved ones again.

In the meantime, know that others are on this path, too, and that you are not alone.

God Bless

About the Author

Marjorie Widmer lives with her husband Kerry on their family farm in the beautiful Windermere Valley, British Columbia, Canada. They love spending time with their daughter Kalie and her partner Greig. This book is taken from her personal experiences and was written with the hope that it bring peace and comfort to others dealing with the loss of a loved one.

Pictures

Kerry, Kalie and myself at Code's memorial bench.

With Code's friends celebrating his 22nd birthday and releasing balloons with messages up to him in heaven.

Our last picture of Code. He had just set up his new XBox. He passed away the next morning.

Our happy family.

Code on his beloved
"Code Red" Dodge 4X4.

Kalie and Code
at his graduation.